Original title:
The Sycamore Sonnets

Copyright © 2025 Creative Arts Management OÜ
All rights reserved.

Author: Dean Whitmore
ISBN HARDBACK: 978-1-80567-375-0
ISBN PAPERBACK: 978-1-80567-674-4

Emotions Intertwined

In a park where oddballs play,
Laughter dances in the day.
Each sycamore, a witness grand,
To funny tales of fire and sand.

A squirrel wears a tiny hat,
As people laugh at this and that.
With ice cream drips and silly cheer,
They jibe at clouds that seem too near.

A jogger trips, it's quite a sight,
His shoelace tied to sheer delight.
The branches sway, they shake their leaves,
As stories tumble, joy achieves.

At sundown, shadows twist and turn,
Forgotten woes just softly burn.
In every sigh, some giggles hide,
With nature's quirk, we take in stride.

Tales from the Rooted Soul

In a garden where secrets grow,
A banana tried to steal the show.
An apple grinned, said, "Oh, my dear,"
"You're just a fruit, I'm the real sphere!"

Lemons laughed, life's sour jest,
While tomatoes claimed to be the best.
But carrots whispered, low and sly,
"We're underground, watching you all fly!"

In the Shade of Time's Passage

Underneath the leafy crown,
A squirrel wore a tiny gown.
It danced around with nuts in hand,
Proclaiming, "I'm the nutty band!"

The wise old owl looked on with glee,
"Those acorns dance like they're on spree!"
He chuckled hard, then took a nap,
While shadows stretched; time's funny trap.

A Canopy of Wild Dreams

A raccoon dreamt of being a star,
While a chickadee flew in bizarre.
He sang so loud, it made birds flee,
"Just return to your nests with glee!"

A cactus rolled his eyes so wide,
"I'm prickly, but let's enjoy the ride!"
With giggles shared among the crowd,
Nature's stage is wild and loud.

The Lilt of Branches and Sky

Branches swayed in a jolly dance,
As clouds all twirled in a playful prance.
A ladybug wore a tiny tie,
"I dress up just to reach the sky!"

The wind played tunes through holes in bark,
While beetles chirped their little lark.
In this world of whimsy and fun,
Nature laughs until the day is done.

The Language of the Leaves

In the breeze, they gossip low,
Telling tales of seeds that grow.
With rustling voices, they conspire,
Sharing stories of sun and fire.

Even squirrels stop to listen tight,
To the chatter of day and night.
A leaf laughs, a twig will tease,
Nature's humor in the trees.

Fertile Conversations

Roots exchange their juicy finds,
While branches wave like chatting blinds.
A sprout whispers to the ground,
As breezes carry laughter round.

Bugs join in with tiny jests,
A merry crew, they love their quests.
In every nook, a laugh or two,
Nature's joy is plain, so true.

Beneath the Whispering Canopy

Shade playfully pokes with dappled light,
As critters giggle in pure delight.
Underneath this leafy dome,
Even mushrooms feel at home.

Branches stretch like arms out wide,
Welcoming all with leafy pride.
To the bees, it's quite the show,
As they buzz around, go with the flow.

A Tapestry of Time

Each ring a tale, each scar a laugh,
Nature weaves her playful craft.
The wind carries secrets, bright and bold,
In the tapestry, stories unfold.

Time plays tricks with shadows long,
As critters dance and sing their song.
A tapestry of fun unspools,
Beneath this grove of leafy fools.

Echoes in the Grove

In a leafy glade, where squirrels dance,
Trees listen closely, to every chance.
A bird sings loud, with quite a flair,
While branches shake, without a care.

The chairs of wood all creak and sigh,
As gossip flows, 'neath open sky.
A raccoon laughs, a little sly,
While shadows stretch, as time drifts by.

A breeze plays tricks on your fine hat,
It flies away, and oh! What a spat!
The flowers giggle in bright array,
As kingfisher dives, to begin the fray.

So gather 'round, the grove is sweet,
With jests and tales, it's quite a treat.
In every rustle, a chuckle waits,
Amongst the trees, where humor baits.

Leaves of Wisdom

A leaf once said, 'Don't take the bait!'
It spiraled down, with a twist so great.
'Life's a quiz, just flip the page,
Find your fun, then take the stage!'

Old trunks remember, in slow replies,
The blush in sunlit, laughing skies.
With acorns dropping, a silly race,
Tiny critters join the chase.

A spider spins, with grand designs,
Turning webs into grand outlines.
Yet every catch is met with grace,
As beetles roll with a funny face.

So gather wisdom, leafy friends,
To joke with clouds, and laughter sends.
In nature's theatre, joy and glee,
Echo the song of being free.

Shadows of Autumn's Embrace

In autumn's glow, shadows play hide,
As pumpkins grin, with seeds inside.
A gust of wind brings laughter loud,
The trees all dance, oh what a crowd!

A fox in red, with a wink so sly,
Chases his tail, oh me, oh my!
Squirrels hoard, then drop their stash,
Hiding acorns in a frantic dash.

Each leaf that falls tells tales of glee,
Of picnics, pies, and friends so free.
The sun dips low, with amber cheer,
While all around, a laugh draws near.

So let's embrace, this season's jest,
With silly hats, we aim for the best.
In shades of amber, we find our chase,
In the autumn's soft, twilight embrace.

Rustic Reverie

In the quiet barn, the cows convene,
With gossip mild, and buttercream.
A rooster crows with utmost pride,
While pigs contently roll and glide.

The scarecrow dons a hat askew,
As the crows plot, their next debut.
Chickens chatter with feathery flair,
While farmers chuckle, without a care.

The old dog snores, mid sunshine beams,
Dreaming of fields and buttered dreams.
The fence post leans, with tales of yore,
While laughter spills from every door.

In rustic charm, we find our peace,
With jokes and joy, let laughter increase.
For in the farm's heart, we weave our thread,
In a vivacious dance, where fun is spread.

Ballad of the Seasonal Travelers

Frogs wear hats in summer's glow,
While squirrels dance in winter's snow.
They swap their stories, trade some glee,
With ice cream cones and cups of tea.

A raccoon plays the tambourine,
While pigeons jive, oh what a scene!
The fox just laughs, with eyes so bright,
In carnival of day and night.

In autumn's breeze, the pumpkins roll,
A marching band of veggie trolls.
They serenade the harvest moon,
While dandelions hum a tune.

So join the fun, don't miss the show,
The seasonal travelers, row by row.
Their laughter rings, a joy parade,
In nature's realm, where pranks are made.

Above and Below: Nature's Conversation

A bird chatters, 'Look at me!',
'I'm flying high, just like a bee!'
A worm retorts, 'I wriggle fine,
Beneath the ground, I sip my wine.'

'You think you're grand, up in the sky?'
Said the spider, hanging high and dry.
'I've got my webs and fancy threads,
While you just fly with silly heads.'

The trees all chuckle, roots sway low,
While clouds roll in, they start the show.
'Can't we all just get along?
Beneath the sun, we all belong!'

Thus nature talks, both high and low,
In whimsical tones, the gossip flows.
A funny dance of words and cheer,
Unites the sky and earth, oh dear!

The Embrace of Earth and Sky

The grass is green, the sky is blue,
But llamas wear shawls—who knew?
With hats of daisies on their heads,
They prance around like little dreads.

The trees wear sunglasses, cool and grand,
While bunnies play in golden sand.
They giggle loud, do cartwheels free,
In this embrace of earth and spree.

Clouds chuckle softly, passing by,
Tickling branches as they fly.
And raindrops burst with giggles bright,
A silly dance in springtime light.

Even the sun can't help but grin,
As nature plays this game of spin.
A raucous ball, where all are friends,
In this embrace that never ends.

Canvas of Seasons' Change

Splashes of color, red and gold,
The trees are artists, brave and bold.
They paint the leaves with laughter's hue,
As winds play tricks, just for a view.

Snowflakes dance in winter's ball,
While rabbits race and squirrels fall.
Each month a canvas, lush and spry,
With nature's brush, we laugh and sigh.

Spring blooms giggle, fresh and bright,
While summer hosts a firefly light.
A festival of sights and sounds,
As nature's art in joy abounds.

Through all the seasons' playful spree,
The world is full of jubilee.
So let us paint with hearts that sing,
In this grand show, our souls on wing.

An Arbor's Story

In the park where I once did stand,
I witnessed mischief, oh so grand.
Squirrels plotting little heists,
Nuts and acorns, their prized feasts.

Children swing and laugh with glee,
I shade them from the summer spree.
Birds who chat away their tales,
About the latest squirrel fails.

With every breeze, my branches sway,
As if to dance the day away.
A poet comes and sits beneath,
To scribble lines, to ponder, breathe.

And when the autumn comes to play,
Leaves like confetti, bright display.
I chuckle softly, watch them twirl,
As all my secrets start to whirl.

The Guardian's Whisper

A giant stands, so wise and bright,
Whispers secrets day and night.
Critters gather, listen near,
To tales of love, and little fear.

Each rustling leaf, a wink and nod,
As if I joke with every prod.
A crow caws loud, thinks he's a star,
But I just chuckle from afar.

Forgetful pigeons, on my skin,
Leave their marks, oh where have you been?
I feel the giggle in the breeze,
As if the wind just took its tease.

When shadows stretch and day is done,
I chuckle at the setting sun.
For in this park, I'm still the king,
Guardian of laughter, welcome spring.

Legacy in the Leaves

In layers thick, my leaves unfold,
Stories hidden, whispers bold.
Many a heart found love in shade,
Memories linger, never fade.

Romantics sit with wine in hand,
Sharing dreams and playful plans.
Yet here I stand, so sturdy still,
Knowing laughter's part of thrill.

Each leaf that falls, a tale of glee,
Of playful winds and wild decree.
But when they dance and fall with grace,
A comic strip, nature's embrace.

So when the autumn's chill creeps in,
And colors burst with cheeky grin,
I wink and wave, oh how they tease,
In laughter's echo, heart at ease.

The Stillness of Stature

In quiet strength, I watch the show,
From sunlit dawn to evening glow.
My roots hold tales of joy and fun,
   Of dusk delights, of races run.

When storms do howl and winds do scream,
I stand my ground, fulfill my dream.
A playground for the sprightly few,
   Yet still the wise in all I do.

Like a jester in a court of green,
I sway with jesters, unseen, unseen.
We toss around the joys of life,
A dance of calm amidst the strife.

So come and sit upon my bark,
And share a laugh, ignite a spark.
For in my stillness, life takes wing,
In humorous shadows, we all sing.

A Symphony of Silence

In the quiet of the night, they snooze,
Crickets play their tunes, while we choose,
To tiptoe 'round the cat, who dreams deep,
Unexpected trysts with mice, oh so steep.

A chorus of snorts, from the comfy chair,
Pillow fights with echoes, filling the air,
Chuckle at shadows dancing on the wall,
Hoping the cookies don't see us at all.

The dog yawns wide, like a lion's roar,
While we sneak some snacks, and try to ignore,
The goldfish judging with bubbles of glee,
As we plot our next heist, just wait and see!

Who knew silence could be this much fun?
As we chuckle softly, our mischief begun,
With every hushed giggle and pillow's embrace,
We revel in quiet, this puzzling race.

Sentinels of the Sky

Balloons fly high, a colorful crew,
Whispering secrets, oh what would they do?
If they spotted a squirrel, plotting its route,
To snatch a stray sandwich, without a doubt.

Pigeons on rooftops, with watchful delight,
Winking at rascals who scurry at night,
They caw and they coo, as if they're in charge,
While we laugh at their antics, thinking it large.

Clouds conspire suspiciously, gathered like friends,
Plotting a rainstorm, which never quite ends,
While sunlight beams down, tickling our toes,
We dance like the grass, in flirty repose.

With giggles and shimmies, we wave to the sky,
As the wind gives a chuckle and whisks us on by,
Every moment unfolds like a comical sight,
In this world of chaos, we revel in flight.

The Art of Stillness

In the park where ducks gobble with haste,
We sit like statues, not wanting to waste,
The perfect moment of sparrows in flight,
While pondering why bread is their favorite bite.

A toddler nearby, with a grin so wide,
Chasing his shadow, with unbridled pride,
While we share a sidelong, bemused little gaze,
At the chaotic simplicity of life's little maze.

Crickets join, doing their nightly ballet,
Each chirp is a laugh that just wants to play,
While we sip lemonade, plotting our schemes,
In this stillness of life, we float on our dreams.

The breeze tickles us, a soft, playful tease,
As we soak in stillness, with giggles and ease,
In the oddest of moments, a joke starts to bloom,
An art form of laughter, in the night's cozy room.

Gazing at the Stars

Under the blanket of glittering light,
We lay like sardines, oh what a sight!
Counting the twinkles, calling them names,
As if they're confetti in interstellar games.

The moon gives a wink, as it juggles the sun,
While we plot to abduct a star just for fun,
Giggles erupt, like a firework show,
As fireworks fade, sprinkled with stardust glow.

Aliens eavesdrop on our giggly spree,
Taking notes on how charming we could be,
With each silly wish that we laugh to confess,
In this cosmic comedy, we find our success.

So if you gaze high, and start to smile wide,
Join our comedy club, let mischief be your guide,
Beneath this film of wonder, we'll share a few laughs,
In our starlit theatre, where joy always drafts.

Secrets in the Bark

Whispers of wind in the trees,
A squirrel's gossip brings us to knees.
Bark-covered tales that twist and turn,
For secrets in nature, we yearn to learn.

The ants hold court on a branch very high,
Debating the best way to fly.
Yet none have wings, what a sight!
Those tiny lawyers, they surely delight!

With roots that tickle and branches that tease,
Sunlight sparkles, a laugh on the breeze.
What stories are etched in that rugged old skin?
Does it know too much, or is it our kin?

As seasons change and the leaves do fall,
The tree just chuckles, it's seen it all.
In a whispering voice, with humor so bright,
The secrets remain, tucked away in the light.

A Canopy of Dreams

Underneath the sprawling green shade,
A world of wishes and games is laid.
Imaginary flights on branches so wide,
A fun little circus where creatures abide.

The raccoons juggle acorns with glee,
While owls hoot jokes from the old oak tree.
Squirrels toss nuts to a tune in the air,
And dance on the branches without any care.

Beyond the twinkle of stars up high,
Dreams pirouette like the fireflies nearby.
A canopy woven from laughter and cheer,
Where every bark scratch is a place to revere.

Here in the woods, where silliness reigns,
The heart finds a rhythm in joy and in pains.
So let's join the party, right under the leaves,
And celebrate life, where mischief conceives.

Songs of the Strongest Tree

The strongest tree sings a wobbly song,
With branches a-dancing, it can't be wrong.
Each leaf a note in a whimsical tune,
Tickling the air like a bright afternoon.

With the wind as its choir, the tree sways and bends,
Creating a melody only nature sends.
Bumblebees buzzing join in for the fun,
While shadows play tag with the rise of the sun.

From roots to the sky, it's both silly and stout,
It chuckles and creaks with a deep, hearty shout.
Old branches will joke, "We're sturdy and wise,"
While tiny grasshoppers leap to the skies.

So spread your branches and sing in delight,
For nature's own laughter brings joy to the night.
The strongest tree knows how to carry a tune,
In the grand concert of life, it shall never be pruned.

Sunlight through the Foliage

Sunlight streams through leaves so bright,
Making shadows dance, oh what a sight!
A disco ball high in the sky,
Where squirrels break out and birds flutter by.

The leaves reveal secrets with a wink,
Their rustling gossip makes us think.
What tales they tell in their vibrant green?
Of woodland antics, quite unforeseen!

Through leaves so thick, the sun drips down,
Making patches of light like a playful crown.
The forest floor is a stage for the bold,
Where stories of laughter in sunlight unfold.

So let's bask in this warmth and cheer,
With sunlight's embrace, we have nothing to fear.
In the dance of the foliage, come take your chance,
And join in the whimsy, the joy, and the dance!

Chronicles of the Ancient Bough

Once a tree, with a grand old grin,
Bore fruit while wearing a leafy chin.
Its branches danced in the sun's bright glee,
Said, "Look at me, I'm as wise as can be!"

When squirrels arrived for an acorn treat,
It shook and giggled beneath their tiny feet.
"Oh, what a ruckus! You're making me sway!"
They laughed as they bounced, and danced away.

With each little breeze, it shared a good tale,
Of how it stood firm through storm and hail.
"Just a tree with a story," it puffed with pride,
"Who'd thought my limbs would be such a ride?"

And so the old bough stood, year after year,
Cracking jokes for all who would hear.
With whispers of wisdom in leaves all aglow,
This ancient fellow, the star of the show!

Swaying with Time

In a park where the people often roam,
A tree tells jokes while its leaves call it home.
"Why don't trees play cards up in the shade?"
"Because they can't stand all the cheques that are made!"

Beneath the bright sun it fluffs its green hair,
Sporting bark that's got stories to share.
"Life's like a dance, with each twist and turn,
You sway to the rhythm while the whole world learns!"

When winter calls in with chilly gusts,
It chuckles and shakes, "This ain't a must!"
"For every snowflake that lands on my limb,
I'll wear it like art, overjoyed and prim!"

As seasons change and the world spins around,
This tree cracks wise, never wears a frown.
With laughter that echoes through wood and through vine,

It keeps on swaying, just having a time!

An Ode to Resilience

Oh mighty tree, who bends but won't break,
In gusty winds, you do a little shake.
"Why struggle so hard to stand so tall?"
"Because falling down is just part of it all!"

When storms come a-knocking, you wave with flair,
Dodging the raindrops, with a shake of your hair.
"Life's like a dance that we didn't choose,
Twist and twirl, you win or you lose!"

A joke in the leaves, a pun in the bark,
Every day you find joy, even after dark.
"Why be a stick in the mud?" you shout,
"Embrace the whole mess, that's what life's about!"

Through laughter and tears, you stand your ground,
Your roots deep in humor, so vast and profound.
With a bark like a chuckle and leaves like a cheer,
You're the jester of woods, oh resilient dear!

From Seed to Majesty

Once a tiny seed with a quirky dream,
Thought it would grow into quite the meme.
"Why aim for grandeur, when I can just be?"
"Let's root for a dance, oh so carefree!"

So sprouted it did, on a sunny old plot,
"Watch me now, I'm a growing big shot!"
With leaf-worthy laughter and humor, quite bright,
It radiated joy, chasing off the night.

As branches reached high, it found some new pals,
Birds sing a tune, and the wind softly cals.
"Is this what it means to be bold and free?
A little bit silly, just happy as can be?"

Now a towering wonder amidst all the fun,
It sways and it jives, with each passing run.
From seed to the sky, what a journey it's paved,
With giggles and grace, oh how it has braved!

Protector of the Quiet Grove

In the grove where squirrels meet,
A guardian stays on tiny feet.
With a cap made of leaves so green,
He rules the realm, a leafy scene.

When the birds come out to play,
He shimmies and shakes in a funny way.
Keeping watch on the acorn stash,
With tiny giggles, he makes a splash.

Beneath branches full of cheer,
He juggles nuts without a fear.
His laughter carried by the breeze,
Tickles the grass and bends the trees.

Oh protector of all that's small,
With a tiny hat, you stand so tall.
In your grove, there's never a frown,
Just playful cheers while the sun goes down.

Underneath the Whispering Canopy

Underneath the leafy dome,
A troupe of critters call it home.
They laugh and dance upon the ground,
In this hideaway, joy knows no bound.

Beneath the branches, stories swirl,
Of dancing mice and a twirling girl.
Every evening, they have a ball,
As fireflies waltz and crickets call.

The wise old owl joins in the fun,
With a silly dance, his work is done.
He teaches moves, makes everyone laugh,
Swinging his wings, he takes a half.

In this place where giggles reign,
Even the rain becomes a game.
So join the party, don't be shy,
Under this canopy, let laughter fly!

Beneath the Old Canopy

Beneath the branches, a festival brews,
With cheeky gnomes in their pointy shoes.
They sneakily snack on sweet little pies,
While dodging the swat from buzzing flies.

Old trees know how to charm and tease,
With shadows that dance in the warm evening breeze.
Each rustling leaf sings a funny tune,
As the moon rises high, they hoot at the moon.

Rabbits in costumes prance around,
With floppy ears bouncing off the ground.
They giggle and hop, and tumble a lot,
In this funny realm, they forget what they're not.

So gather your friends, pull up a seat,
Join in the laughter—oh, what a treat!
Under this canopy, joy takes flight,
With silly shadows into the night.

Whispers of the Branches

Whispers float from twig to twig,
As critters below dance a jig.
Frogs in bowties leap with glee,
As squirrels spin tales of their spree.

The old tree chuckles, holds its ground,
With stories that make the grass resound.
All the branches share their tales,
Of secret quests and feathered sails.

In this place of playful rhyme,
They banter and joke, it's laughter's time.
A bumblebee buzzes, with a cheeky grin,
"Shall we dance? Let the fun begin!"

So if you wander into this glade,
Prepare for laughter, a grand parade.
For underneath these intertwining strands,
Are giggles and cheers, and dancing hands.

Whispers of the Old Tree

In a park where old trees stand,
Squirrels chatter, quite unplanned.
Branches sway with a silly dance,
As leaves gossip in a leafy prance.

Beneath the shade, a picnic spread,
With ants marching, dreams misled.
A sandwich fights with a playful breeze,
As juice boxes float like tiny seas.

An owl hoots with a quirky twist,
While children giggle, they can't resist.
A raccoon peeks with a cheeky grin,
As laughter bubbles, chaos begins.

Sunshine spills like golden paint,
On the trunks where laughter's quaint.
Around the tree, life's a hoot,
With funny tales that are absolute.

Shadows Beneath the Boughs

In the shade where shadows play,
A frog leaps oddly, comes what may.
Twigs snap under feet that slip,
Each misstep leads to a giggling trip.

A dog chases a butterfly's flight,
While kids shriek with sheer delight.
The tree stands tall, a watchful eye,
On every jest and every sigh.

Beneath the leaves, the whispers tease,
A breeze carries tales with such ease.
Jokes fly like acorns in the sun,
In this realm, we all have fun.

With shadows dancing on the ground,
Laughter echoes all around.
In boughs above, mischief brews,
Among the leaves, the humor stews.

Songs of the Hollow Heart

In a trunk so wide and deep,
A squirrel stashes nuts for keeps.
With each thud, a comical thrum,
Echoes of laughter, oh what fun!

A woodpecker taps a lively beat,
While woodland critters all take a seat.
They sing of mishaps and silly flops,
Telling tales till the laughter stops.

A hedgehog rolls, clad in spines,
While rabbits dance in silly lines.
The heart of the tree, alive with cheer,
Every whimsy brings joy near.

Hollow heart, a drum of joy,
Filling the air, a giggling ploy.
In nature's choir, we all play our part,
Singing the songs from the hollow heart.

Echoes of Autumn's Embrace

Autumn's leaves in colors bright,
Twirl down in a comical flight.
They tickle noses, dance on heads,
As nature laughs in golden threads.

A pumpkin rolls with a happy bounce,
While kids giggle and jump in pounce.
Scarecrows lean with a lopsided grin,
Guarding cornfields where fun begins.

Crisp air carries a playful tease,
As kites soar, caught in the breeze.
Each gust brings a silly surprise,
With laughter soaring to the skies.

Echoes of joy in the harvest hue,
Fill the fields and the skies so blue.
In autumn's dance, we find our grace,
In every moment, we embrace the chase.

Beneath the Guardian's Gaze

Under branches wide and green,
Squirrels dance and chase unseen.
A guardian high, with leafy crown,
Watches antics, never frown.

To his left, a chipmunk prances,
Counting acorns, taking chances.
A breeze whispers of playful days,
As shadows jig in leafy play.

Beneath the gaze so wise and sly,
A choir of critters flit and fly.
Every rustle, a song of cheer,
Nature's laughs ring crystal clear.

Oh, to be a leaf in flight,
Twisting, turning, pure delight.
With each gust, a giggle shared,
Beneath the glance, none are scared!

The Ballet of Petals in Spring

Petals pirouette on the breeze,
Dancing down with greatest ease.
A flower's frock in colors bright,
Startles bees in sheer delight.

The wind, a director, takes the lead,
As blossoms flutter, swirl, and heed.
With every twist, a pollen flight,
Twirling bees take joyful bite.

Grass blades serve as stage so green,
Nature's theater, rarely seen.
Round and round, they frolic about,
In this ballet, none have doubt.

As springtime blooms a vibrant tale,
Watch the petals sail, never pale.
In a riot of colors, life does spring,
You can't help but laugh; it's a joyous thing!

Memory of the Seasons' Breath

Seasons whisper through the leaves,
A chorus echoes, if one believes.
Winter chuckles; ice does crack,
While spring sneezes—'Ah, bless that!'

Summer struts with golden glow,
And autumn laughs as breezes blow.
Each memory, a giggling sprite,
As colors fade to cozy night.

Oh, how they share their funny ways,
Chasing sunlight, counting days.
A tapestry of laughs and cheers,
Through the cycle, spanning years.

With every turn of the seasons' wheel,
Nature's humor is the real deal.
In every rustle, a chuckle found,
In evergreen's grasp, joy abounds!

Soliloquy of the Bark

Bark speaks softly, tales untold,
Of windy nights and sun so bold.
A sage of wood, with stories grand,
Of playful sprigs and animal band.

Here's a tale of a daring crow,
Stealing berries with a bow.
Oh how the squirrels tease and shout,
While woodpeckers dance about!

The years roll on; it's quite absurd,
To hear a tree speak every word.
In knots and grooves, life's quirkiness,
A bark's soliloquy, pure silliness.

Laughing leaves fall to ground below,
As whispers rise, and breezes blow.
In nature's script, we all play part,
Humbly acknowledged by the bark's heart!

Dance of Leaves in Twilight

In twilight's glow, the leaves all prance,
Like clowns in trees, a leafy dance.
They twist and twirl in breezy glee,
Inviting us to join, come see!

With every rustle, laughter gleams,
The branches giggle, so it seems.
A squirrel joins with leaps and bounds,
Creating chaos in the sounds!

The shadows stretch, they stretch and sway,
While acorns fall, an aerial play.
Nature's jesters, wild and free,
Invite the night to laugh with glee!

So as we watch this leafy show,
Let's join the dance, let go, let go!
For life's a stage with trees galore,
With every leaf, we ask for more!

The Canopy of Dreams

Under the trees, where dreams collide,
A canopy where squirrels slide.
The branches wave like hands on air,
Whispering secrets without a care.

While down below, the shadows creep,
We hear the giggles of dreams that leap.
A raccoon winks with mischief bright,
As stars peek through in sheer delight.

The owls in jest, with eyes so wide,
Tell tales of nonsense with great pride.
They hoot in rhythm, a comical tune,
While night unfolds beneath the moon.

So if you're lost, just look above,
At dreams and laughter, filled with love.
In this leafy haven, we'll always find,
A canopy of joy intertwined!

Secrets of the Twisted Branch

In a twisted branch, secrets are spun,
A hidden world where mischief's begun.
The woodpecker taps, a funny beat,
While shadows chuckle beneath our feet.

Squirrels debate the best nut to stash,
Congregating like a laughing clash.
While raccoons grin, they can't help but sneak,
All sharing tales that make us squeak!

The branches bend and sway, oh so coy,
In this realm of roots, mischief's the joy.
What wonders bloom beneath each bark,
As twilight lingers in the dark.

With every secret that whispers and sighs,
Nature presents its clever disguise.
So whisper back, let laughter dance,
In the twisted branch, give joy a chance!

Chronicles of the Whispering Wind

The wind tells tales with whispers sweet,
Of dancing leaves and nimble feet.
It tickles branches, makes them sway,
In a frolicsome rush, come join the play!

Each gust of breeze brings laughter near,
As trees confess what they hold dear.
From stories of love to jokes of trees,
The wind brings joy on a playful breeze.

Beneath the boughs, secrets abound,
With plucky birds and critters around.
They chirp and chime in a merry choir,
Singing songs that never tire.

So listen close, let laughter entwine,
In the chronicles of wind's sweet line.
For every sigh and giggle caught,
Brings forth a tale that can't be bought!

Parables in the Bark

A tree once told a joke so fine,
Its leaves fell down, but who could whine?
Squirrels giggled, birds took flight,
In the wood, laughter danced so bright.

Woodpecker made a tap-tap cheer,
Echoing tales we love to hear.
Photosynthesis, a wild affair,
The sun's my friend, I love to share!

Bark's thick skin with patterns swirled,
Each ring a secret, each knot unfurled.
When branches chat, they twist and bend,
Nature's humor knows no end.

So when you walk through trees so fine,
Listen close — there's jokes divine!
Nature's punchlines, bright and clear,
In harmony, we all can cheer.

The Heartbeat of the Forest

In the glade where whispers play,
The trees dance to a funny sway.
Roots tap-tap on the ground,
A rhythm that's silly and profound.

A frog croaks out a comedic song,
While rabbits hop, as if they belong.
Critters clothed in nature's attire,
Their antics spark woodland fire!

Trees wear hats of mossy green,
A forest full of quirky scene.
Saplings giggle; they're short but spry,
In the sun where the birds fly high.

Old logs tell tales 'round the bend,
Where laughter echoes, without end.
The forest beats, a joyful jest,
A playful heart that never rests.

Life's Branching Paths

In life we branch, just like a tree,
Choosing paths like squirrels with glee.
Twists and turns do make us laugh,
As we tumble through nature's draft.

A fox took left, a mouse went right,
They tripped on roots — oh, what a sight!
Paths crisscross like noodles in play,
In every moment, joy will stay!

Birds circling high, maps yet to unfold,
Each branch ahead, a story bold.
Leaves might fall, but spirits soar,
In life's great maze, there's always more.

With every twist, a chuckle's found,
Nature's playground, joyful and round.
Finding our way, with humor intact,
Life's branching paths, a whimsical act.

Eloquent Roots

Beneath the ground, the roots collide,
In whispers soft, they jive and bide.
A tongue-tied vine, so eloquent,
Spreads tales of joy, so well-meant.

Gathering dirt like gossip shared,
With every tickle, the ground is aired.
Worms chuckle, dances in play,
Fungi giggle in their grand display!

Roots spread wide, a funny team,
With all their twists, they live the dream.
Holding stories of the earth,
With a punchline that gives them worth.

Beneath the surface lies the fun,
Where life begins, and games are spun.
Each root a belly laugh from below,
In forest depths, the laughter flows.

In the Shade of Ages

Under broad branches, we tell our tales,
Squirrels listen, they raise their sails.
With acorn hats, they dance about,
While we laugh and try not to spout.

A jay caws loudly, thinks he's the bard,
Critiquing our art, oh how it's hard!
Leaves whisper secrets, they know our flaws,
Yet here in the shade, it's all 'round of applause.

Chasing the shadows, we'll do the jig,
With grass for a stage, we're all feeling big.
A worm in the mud, he joins the fun,
In this leafy realm, we're all number one.

As sunset sneaks, we stretch our backs,
Swapping our stories, some winged they lack.
Laughter erupts in this timeless space,
Under ages-old boughs with smiles on each face.

Harmony in the Heartwood

In a trunk's embrace, we found our tune,
A chorus of crickets, under the moon.
Branches sway gently, they join the show,
A concert of whispers in breezy flow.

With laughter as notes, we sing with glee,
A tickled tree frog joins in, you see.
With every new verse, a branch bends down,
Trying to catch the giggles we crown.

The earth taps its roots, keeping the beat,
As squirrels stage dive, what a feat!
The flowers join in, with their petals spread,
In harmony thriving, we dance, we shred.

So here in this wood, our voices collide,
A playful alliance, where hearts can slide.
With the stars above, we take a bow,
In nature's orchestra, we sing 'live now'.

Nature's Lullaby

Under the canopy, birds croon slow,
While a chipmunk snores, dreaming of snow.
The brook hums a tune, soft as a sigh,
A serenade sweet, as time flutters by.

Moss blankets the ground, plush as a bed,
Snuggled in greens, we rest our head.
With laughter turned whispers, the sun fades away,
And fireflies glitter like stars in the fray.

A raccoon sneaks in, thinking he's sly,
Mistaken for quiet, he bumps and he cries.
While shadows grow longer, we hear the night hum,
In nature's embrace, we'll all stay numb.

As dreams drift to us from the treetop vault,
Critters convene with a chuckle, a halt.
With the moon as our blanket, we softly sway,
In the lull of the woods, we frolic and play.

The Lure of the Leaf

A leaf on the wind, it twirls with delight,
Chasing squirrels around, oh what a sight!
With acrobat antics, they zoom and they spin,
While we crack up laughing, let the fun begin.

Fluffy clouds drift, dancing through blue,
While down at our feet, ladybugs queue.
With tiny red coats, they march in a line,
While we pretend to be their great design.

The grass tickles toes, they giggle and squeal,
Worms peek from the soil, what's their deal?
They wiggle and twist, with mischief they plot,
While we muse over snacks and chirp on the spot.

Beneath boughs of laughter, we gather our cheer,
As twilight draws near, and fireflies appear.
In the lure of green, we find our reprieve,
With each silly moment, we learn to believe.

Tales of the Tall

Once I met a tree so grand,
With branches stretching, they would stand.
I asked it for a word or two,
It shook its leaves and said, "Boo-hoo!"

All the squirrels, they laughed so loud,
It made me feel quite silly, proud.
'You think you're tall?' one chirped with glee,
'You're just a puny, stumpy he!'

Under its shade, I wanted to play,
But ants marched on, they had their way.
They flipped my cap, ran off with cheer,
That tree just chuckled, "I'm not a deer!"

So now I sit beneath its reign,
With tales of giants, winks of pain.
In this green kingdom, I'll forever dwell,
A tiny jester in a leafy spell!

Murmurs of the Meadow

In the meadow where daisies twirl,
Stood a flower, bright and a swirl.
It whispered secrets, soft and low,
'You think there's sun? Oh, you should know!'

A bumblebee buzzed, wearing a frown,
'Why'd I choose this lumbering crown?'
It crashed into clover, lost all grace,
Then made a joke about 'Pollen Face.'

Nearby, a snail deemed itself quite fast,
Said, 'I'm a rocket when I blast!'
The daisies giggled, swayed in sync,
'Oh really, dear? Let's see you think!'

In this laughter, joy does blossom,
Where tiny critters bring cheer and possum.
Each leaf and petal takes a chance,
In the meadow's funny, dancy dance!

In the Presence of Giants

Beside the oaks so big and wide,
I slipped on acorns, took a slide.
The trees looked down with mighty eyes,
'Is that a squirrel or just my prize?'

One barked loud like it was a joke,
While I lay flat without a poke.
I raised my head, tried hard to grin,
'You think you're tough? Let's have a spin!'

The branches swayed, they seemed to sigh,
'We've seen many tumble, oh my, oh my!'
But laughing echoes filled the air,
As I tumbled twice then stood with flair.

In this grand world of bark and leaf,
I felt so tiny but full of grief.
Yet laughter reigned in nature's hall,
For even giants can have a fall!

A Treetop's Perspective

Up above the world so wide,
I clung to branches, felt the glide.
A bird called out, said, 'Try this view!'
'See all the folks, and who are you?'

I waved to people busy below,
They looked so tiny, moving slow.
A cloud drifted near, gave me a nudge,
'Hey up there, don't you dare budge!'

The wind then whispered, 'A joke, a jest!'
'You think you're high? I'll make this test!'
Just as it said, a breeze gave a push,
With a giggle, I was in a rush!

Treetops chuckled, swayed with glee,
While below, people searched for me.
From this height, humor's golden thread,
In leafy laughter, I would tread!

Glimmers of Time

In a world where seconds tick,
The clock's a mischievous trick.
It jumps ahead, then lags behind,
A playful dance, so unconfined.

With each chime, the cats retreat,
Chasing shadows, what a feat!
The dog just snoozes, quite unfazed,
While time juggles, all amazed.

Sunset giggles, morning yawns,
Hiding from the break of dawn.
We laugh and skip, we trip and fall,
As minutes play with one and all.

In the end, with smiles so wide,
We bend the rules, can't let them slide.
A world of jest and ticklish rhyme,
In our hearts, we bide our time.

Under Twilight's Gaze

Beneath the stars, the crickets hum,
While fireflies dance, they're quite the drum.
The moon winks with a cheeky grin,
As night unfolds, let the jokes begin.

A raccoon steals snacks from the picnic spread,
While the owl hoots, 'What's the deal?', they said.
The raccoon laughs, with crumbs in paws,
This midnight feast deserves applause!

Twilight chuckles, a sight to see,
As shadows play hide and seek with glee.
Nature twirls in a silly trance,
Underneath, the stars all prance.

As dreams unfold with ladybugs,
And laughter spreads in cozy hugs.
We tiptoe softly, what a maze,
Creating memories under twilight's gaze.

Nature's Timekeepers

The trees whisper secrets in the breeze,
Like old friends sharing timeless tease.
A squirrel dashes, quite the spry,
While nature sings, 'Just say hi!'

Flowers bloom without a care,
Playing dress-up everywhere.
With petals spinning, colors bright,
Nature giggles, what a sight!

The river flows in a silly way,
Splashing laughter every day.
While frogs croak jokes from lily pads,
Keeping spirits high, and no one's sad.

The sun peeks through leaves with a wink,
Casting shadows that dance and clink.
Nature's clock ticks with endless cheer,
Come join the laughter, all are welcome here!

Portraits of Green

In the gallery of leaves so bright,
Painted by the sun's soft light.
Each blade of grass, a brushstroke fine,
Crafting giggles, one of a kind.

Dandelions puff, like old gumdrops,
As busy bees buzz, over the crops.
"Hurry!" they say, "Time's a funny thing!"
"It's gold!" they'll buzz, on a bee-shaped wing.

Trees pose proudly, keeping score,
As squirrels come in, seeking more.
With acorns tucked beneath a grin,
Life's silly canvas, where joys begin.

With each shade and twist of hue,
Nature giggles: 'Look at you!'
These portraits tell of laughter's reign,
In a world so weird, full of green terrain.

The Legacy of Leaf and Sky

A leaf fell down with a quirk,
Declared it's now a piece of art.
Each breeze it caught did a smirk,
Got tangled up in a branchy part.

The squirrels gathered and they sighed,
For winter's chill was in the air.
Yet, they all danced with silly pride,
Who knew that leaves could cause such flair?

A sunny day, a shadow's game,
The branches waved, it seemed absurd.
With every gust, it yelled its name,
Promising a fluttered word.

So here's to trees with their own style,
Creating laughter, joy, and jest.
Forever we'll remember their smile,
For nature's love is always best.

Reveries among the Twisting Trunks

Beneath the trunks, the wisdom lies,
With tales of nuts and acorn fights.
They laugh and giggle in disguise,
While branches twist like tangled lights.

A turtle came to join the fun,
Claimed he could beat a leaf in flight.
But on his back, he could not run,
And ended up in quite a plight.

The shadows stretched, the laughter soared,
As woodland creatures joined the lore.
Each twist and turn, a jest was scored,
Filling the air with giggles galore.

With every turn, the forest boomed,
A symphony of playful cheer.
For in this grove, no heart was doomed,
Where friends abound, there's nothing to fear.

An Invitation to the Woodland Dance

The forest floor is dressed in gold,
An invitation on the breeze.
Let's dance until the night is old,
With critters swaying 'neath the trees.

The rabbits hop with joyful glee,
While owls spin tales up in the dark.
Each twirl is free, a wild decree,
Even the crickets sing their spark.

The moon peeks down, a watchful eye,
While mushrooms twirl with mischievous flair.
We dizzy dance and lift up high,
In reverie, we have not a care.

So gather round, come one, come all,
To woodland's beat, we shall entrust.
A jolly joy, we'd never stall,
To dance till day breaks with a rust!

Reflections of the Seasons' Endeavor

The autumn leaves begin to play,
They whirl and twirl like tiny kites.
While winter watches from far away,
With chilly breath and frosty bites.

It grinned and waved as spring arrived,
With buds that giggled as they bloomed.
In each new bloom, the world revived,
And all of nature soon resumed.

Oh summer laughed with muddy feet,
As puddles formed and splashes flew.
Each season brought its own heartbeat,
Creating joy in skies so blue.

So raise a glass to nature's game,
For every twist a jest unfolds.
With seasons changing, nothing's the same,
And laughter's worth more than mere gold.

In the Shade of Memory

Beneath the leaves where secrets hide,
I remember a time when I nearly cried.
A squirrel once stole my sandwich straight,
I chased it around, but it laughed at fate.

Those branches swayed, a comedy show,
As I tripped on roots, oh how low I go!
Laughter echoed through the sunny glade,
While nature chuckled, never afraid.

The sunbeams danced on the forest floor,
While my antics failed to win any score;
Yet the trees stood tall with their leafy cheer,
Reminding me that joy is always near.

So here I sit, nostalgia's embrace,
With nothing but laughter adorning my face.
In the shade of memory, I'll always roam,
For in this laughter, I find my home.

Nature's Quiet Strength

In the quiet woods, a frog sings loud,
Croaking out tunes to impress the crowd.
With leaps so grand, he takes the stage,
Performing for mice without turning a page.

A breeze blows in, tickles the leaves,
The trees giggle softly, as if they believe.
Each acorn drops like laughter from high,
As squirrels scurry on, oh my, oh my!

Roots intertwined, a tangled mess,
Nature's strength shines, no need to impress.
Even the ants hold a dance in their stride,
While the plants nod along, full of pride.

Under the boughs, life finds its way,
With funny mishaps brightening the day.
Nature's quiet strength, a comic dance,
Where every critter gets its chance.

Generations of Growth

In a twisted trunk, stories unwind,
Of moments and memories, every kind.
The old tree chuckles, wise as a sage,
While its saplings giggle, setting the stage.

The younger ones stretch, reaching for light,
Tripping on grass, what a clumsy sight!
One leaf asked another, "Am I too green?"
"It's all in your head; we're the best that's been!"

The roots like a family, stubborn and bold,
Growing together, as each tale unfolds.
They tease each other with jokes quite absurd,
While the wind whispers sweetly, never disturbed.

Generations pass, yet the laughter remains,
In every bark line, in sunshine and rains.
Together they thrive, through thick and through thin,
With nature's own humor, vibrant within.

The Wisdom of the Woods

In the heart of the forest, a wise old owl,
Perched on a branch, makes quite the growl.
He hoots out advice, not always sound,
Like how to woo squirrels, or dig underground.

The wise trees nod, their leaves all a'quiver,
As the wind wraps around, like a playful river.
"Owl, you old joker, what do you know?"
He just winks back, "Sit tight, and grow!"

"Leave your worries, let laughter abide,
For juggling acorns always offers a ride.
When branches shake, it's not just the breeze,
It's nature's giggles, put your mind at ease."

So next time you stroll through the tall, leafy maze,
Listen for laughter in these wooded bays.
The wisdom of the woods, a lighthearted tune,
A reminder that joy can be found every noon.

The Dance of the Wind

Breezes shimmy, twirl, and sway,
Playing tag with clouds today.
Whispers tickle bark and boughs,
The trees laugh, let's take a bow!

Squirrels spin in dizzying glee,
Windswept acorns roll like a bee.
Branches wave, a wacky crew,
Even the roots join in, too!

A tumble here, a giggle there,
Nature's dance, light as the air.
Watch the grass hop, what a sight,
As sunlight fades, they take flight!

With every gust, a story's spun,
Of woodland pranks and silly fun.
When wind takes center stage, we find,
Laughter echoes, so unconfined.

Soliloquy of the Leaves

Leaves chatter loudly, don't be shy,
They gossip softly, wink an eye.
"Did you see the squirrel miss?"
"Oh, please! Spare me that sweet bliss!"

One tree tickles another friend,
With swaying limbs, till branches bend.
"I've got a secret, listen close,
I saw a crow perform a pose!"

They joke about the rain that falls,
Who wears the best and friendliest shawls?
Each raindrop is a playful tease,
A splash, a giggle, among the trees.

With every flutter, tales unfold,
In hues of green, worth more than gold.
Nature's comic troupe, always in play,
Leaves confer until the end of day.

Seasons' Silent Watch

The seasons chuckle, keep a score,
As blooms burst forth from winter's door.
Spring promises with a wink and grin,
While summer's heat makes eye frames spin.

Autumn enters with a crunch and sway,
Leaves drop down, they dance, they play.
Winter snickers at the trees all bare,
As snowflakes tickle without a care.

Each season whispers, playful and sly,
With nature's antics, how time can fly!
Moments frozen in a gusty breeze,
Life is lighter 'neath swaying trees.

They watch in silence as time goes round,
But laughter echoes, a joyful sound.
Nature's jesters, a whimsical lot,
A ballet of seasons, a funny plot.

Roots of Remembrance

Roots hold tales from days gone by,
They chuckle softly, say, 'Oh my!'
Each twist and turn, a memory made,
Of mice who danced in the evening shade.

Beneath the soil, where secrets flow,
They murmur, 'Do you remember Joe?'
The raccoon who thought he could hide,
Yet tripped on vines, oh, the pride!

Digging deep, they share their lore,
Whispers of the forest floor.
In tangled knots, how friendships grow,
Their timeless tales, forever aglow.

While branches sway above, so spry,
Roots keep laughing, as time slips by.
With every gust, another jest,
In nature's heart, they're truly blessed.

Flickers of Sunlight

In the morning light, birds chirp and tease,
While squirrels dance, moving with ease.
The leaves laugh softly, rustle and sway,
As sunlight plays games in a bright ballet.

A shadow sneaks in, a cat on the prowl,
Valiantly failing with a clumsy growl.
It trips on a root, with a fumble and flail,
And the trees all chuckle, a warm gust of hail.

All around, nature's humor shines bright,
With critters and branches, a delightful sight.
They flip and they flop while I sip my tea,
In this wacky circus, it's just them and me.

So here's to the trees, the jesters of air,
With stories they whisper, a playful affair.
Flickers of sunlight, oh what a show,
Living with laughter, a marvelous glow.

Earthbound Elegy

Roots stretch beneath, in a tangled embrace,
As worms do their dance, at a slow, silly pace.
I watch them wiggle, so serious and wise,
They loop in circles, a grand little prize.

With the earth's hidden chorus, I can't help but laugh,
As ants plot their journeys, they form a new path.
A squirrel nearby is just barking up trees,
While dandelions puff and sway in the breeze.

The snails take it slow, with plans that are grand,
As they carry their homes like a tiny bandstand.
Each creature plays part in this comical play,
As I join the fun, watching night turn to day.

So here's to the soil, rich with mirth and jest,
Where even the smallest find joy and invest.
An earthbound elegy, spun with delight,
We'll dance in the dirt 'til the end of the night.

The Cycles of Canopy

Up in the branches, squirrels plot and scheme,
As little acrobats chase the soft beams.
The canopy rustles with giggles and glee,
While leaves eavesdrop on secrets, you see.

A beetle gets stuck, a grand tale to tell,
As it wiggles and squiggles, caught in a spell.
The whispers of winds tease them to roam,
But humus and petunias call them back home.

Sunlight peeks down with mischievous flair,
Playing hide and seek through the forested air.
In this merry dance, jests rise and fall,
Nature's own laughter, a grand free-for-all.

So raise up your glass to the birds and the trees,
Who've spun this wild laughter upon playful breeze.
Cycles of canopy, where joy finds its way,
In a world of green jesters, come join in the play.

Kinship with the Earth

Listen close to the soil, it giggles and sighs,
With roots that entwine in the silliest ties.
Frogs croak their verses in playful refrain,
While daisies nod knowingly, sweet as champagne.

With every soft breeze, I can hear the trees laugh,
As they sway in delight, crafting nature's own chaff.
A rabbit hops over, quite proud of its show,
While earthworms are grinning, as all critters know.

Under moonlit nights, the crickets compose,
With a symphony croaked from their tiny repose.
The world has a rhythm, a beat full of mirth,
In this joyful pastel, my kinship with Earth.

So gather 'round, friends, in the forest we'll play,
With the humor of nature, we'll dance night and day.
In friendship with flora and fauna's warm cheer,
Let's laugh with the earth, it's abundantly clear!

Embracing the Essence

In a forest of laughs, trees tell their tales,
With branches that dance like they're on trails.
Squirrels wear ties, quite a sight to behold,
As they barter for acorns, or so they are told.

The leaves gossip softly, with rustling cheer,
About antics of owls who can't keep a leer.
"Why did the pine jest?" quips a cheeky sprout,
"Because it wanted to be a tad pined out!"

Bark-clad comedians, they take center stage,
In a stand-up routine that never will age.
With roots intertwined, in laughter they bask,
Just don't ask the maple; it's shy, not a flack.

So gather around, let the giggles arise,
As nature's oddities throw jokes that surprise.
Among the green giants, the foolish and free,
Life's pun-filled parade is forever a spree.

Reflections Underneath

Beneath the old boughs, a mirror has grown,
Where the critters engage in a fight they've outgrown.
"The grass is greener," the rabbit once said,
As he peered at his rival, a well-groomed thread.

The toads in tuxedos play hopscotch with flair,
While the fish in the pond gossip without a care.
"What do you call a frog with no legs?" they croak,
"Unhoppy, I fear!" is the heartfelt joke.

With giggles aplenty and water so clear,
Nature's reflections spread laughter, not fear.
Sunlight must chuckle, as shadows they tease,
While the weeping willow sways in the breeze.

Beneath the old boughs, joy knows no bounds,
With tales spinning laughter from hidden surrounds.
The forest puts on its best jester's cap,
In reflections so silly, we take a long nap.

The Soul of Olden Timber

We've got an old tree, wise and full of jest,
Who knows all the secrets that nature confessed.
He chuckles and creaks, with each little breeze,
Telling tales of the past with the utmost ease.

"Why was the wood glad?" he humorously posed,
"Because it finally found where its humor stemmed and dozed!"
The squirrels rolled over, their sides nearly split,
As branches wiggled with every cheeky bit.

Underneath the crown, where the shadows do play,
The roots whisper secrets in a curious way.
Time holds no pressure when laughter's at stake,
As the old timber grins, never a break.

The soul of this tree sings about the fun,
Of seasons and pranks underneath the warm sun.
So join in the laughter, let worries take flight,
And dance with the spirits that twinkle at night.

Sighs of the Seasons

Autumn brings chuckles in colors so bright,
As leaves wiggle down in a playful fright.
The squirrels prepare, with a hoard and a plan,
To pick on the pumpkins, oh yes, they are fans!

Winter sneaks in, with its frosty, white pranks,
Snowmen conspire, as they fill with blank ranks.
"Do you hear what I hear?" the robin does tease,
"A snowball's a treat, only if it's freeze!"

Spring softly croons with a tickle of cheer,
As buds burst with laughter, and flowers appear.
The bees buzz their songs, while the daisies sway,
Life dances anew, taking gloom far away.

And summer arrives with a burst of delight,
As picnics abound, and the sun shines so bright.
Each season a chapter, where giggles ignite,
Nature's funny book, a whimsical light.

www.ingramcontent.com/pod-product-compliance
Lightning Source LLC
Chambersburg PA
CBHW071838160426
43209CB00003B/336